The Swiftie Dictionary: A guide to Taylor Swift's songs
Naomi Curl

I0783862

To Mother
To Mom

Aa

Abigail: Refers to Swift's lifelong best friend, Abigail Anderson Berard (née Lucier), whom she met in high school.

Achilles heel: A point of weakness.

Acid rock: Rock music with lyrics and sound relating to or suggestive of drug-induced experiences.

Acrobat: One adept at swiftly changing or adapting to a position or viewpoint.

Adorned: To enliven or decorate with ornaments.

Aesthetic: Concerned with beauty or the appreciation of beauty.

Allegiance: Loyalty or commitment of an individual to a group or cause.

Afflicted: Suffering from pain, distress or disability.

Afterglow: Light or radiance remaining in the sky after the sun has set. Good feelings that remain after a pleasurable or successful experience.

Aftermath: The period immediately following a usually ruinous event.

Albatross: A very large oceanic bird related to the shearwaters, with long narrow wings. A source of frustration or guilt.

Alchemy: The medieval forerunner of chemistry, based on the supposed transformation of matter. It was concerned particularly with attempts to convert base metals into gold or to find a universal elixir.

All's well that ends well: An expression meaning that if the outcome of a situation is happy, this compensates for any previous difficulty or unpleasantness. A play by William Shakespeare.

Alpha type: Dominant male type.

Altruism: Selfless concern for the well-being of others, without caring about one's own interests.

Amateur: One lacking in experience and competence.
American Pie: Coming of age movie released in 1999.
Angel's City: Refers to Los Angeles, California.
Anoint: To put oil on someone as part of a religious ceremony. To officially or formally choose someone to do or be something.
Anthology: A published collection of poems or other pieces of writing. Refers to Taylor's TTPD bonus album released in 2024.
Anti-hero: A central character in a story, movie, or drama who lacks conventional heroic attributes.
Antithetical: directly opposed or contrasted; mutually incompatible.
Archer: A person who uses a bow and arrow.
Argumentative: Given to expressing divergent or opposite views.
Aristotle: Greek philosopher and scientist. He is one of the most influential thinkers in the history of Western thought.
Arson: The criminal act of deliberately setting fire to property.
Artifacts: An object made or modified by a human being, typically one of cultural or historical interest.
Asylum: Shelter or protection from danger. An institution for the care of people with mental illness.
A-team: An elite or expert group comprising those who are most pre-eminent in an organization, profession, or activity.
Aurora Borealis: A natural electrical phenomenon characterized by the appearance of streamers of reddish or greenish light in the sky also referred to as Northern Lights.
A Wrinkle in Time: A novel written by Madeleine L 'Engle, which follows a 13-year-old girl as she journeys through space and time.

Bb

Backlogged: Accumulated unperformed task or materials not processed.

Bait and Switch: The ploy of offering a person something desirable to gain favor, then thwarting expectations with something less desirable.

Bad blood: Feeling of ill will, anger or hostility between people.

Balenci: A shorthand for Balenciaga, the luxury fashion house known for avant-garde designs.

Baren: Bleak and lifeless. Empty of meaning or value.

Beguiling: Charming or enchanting, often in a deceptive way.

Bejeweled: Decorated or as if with jewels.

Benz: Mercedez Benz, a German luxury car.

Bereft: Suffering the death of a loved one. Lacking something needed, wanted, or expected.

Bestow: To convey as a gift.

Beverly Hills: A city located in Los Angeles, California.

Bewitching: Enchanting or delightful.

Billows: A large undulating mass of something, typically cloud, smoke, or steam.

Bluff: A false threat or claim intended to deter or deceive someone.

Bobby: In the song Starlight, Bobby refers to Robert F. Kennedy who was married to Ethel Kennedy.

Bolter: A person or animal that bolts or runs away.

Bond Street: Located in the West End of London, it is considered the home of luxury shopping in London.

Bonnie and Clyde: American bandits and serial killers who traveled the Central United States with their gang during the Great Depression.

Boss up: Slang for stepping into power and confidence, often used in hip-hop to mean elevating one's status or mindset.

Brink: an extreme edge of land before a steep or vertical slope. A point at which something, typically something unwelcome, is about to happen, the verge.

Brixton: An area in South London.

Burgundy: A deep red color like that of Burgundy wine.

Burton: Richard Burton, actor who was married twice to actress Elizabeth Taylor.

Bury the hatchet: To forgive or to make peace; an allusion to the practice of putting weapons away.

Byline: A line at the beginning of a news story, magazine article, or book giving the writer's name.

Cc

Cad: A low-bred, presuming person; a mean, vulgar fellow, especially one that cannot be trusted with a lady.
Calamitous: Catastrophic or disastrous.
Calloused: Having an area of hardened skin, usually due to overuse.
Cartier: The prestigious French jewelry brand famous for luxury watches and gems like the Love Bracelet.
Cassandra: Ancient Trojan priestess who was fated to be a prophet but was never believed, most famously about Greek troops hiding inside the Trojan Horse.
Camden Market: A number of adjoining large retail markets, often collectively referred to as Camden Market or Camden Lock, located in Camden Town, London.
Cascade: A waterfall or series of small waterfalls. A succession of devices or stages in a process, each of which triggers or initiates the next one.
Catastrophic: Involving or causing sudden great damage or suffering.
Centennial Park: Centennial Park is a large urban park located approximately two miles west of downtown Nashville, Tennessee.
Centerfold: The single larger sheet of paper that forms the middle two pages of a magazine or other publication, folded to open wider than a standard page spread.
Champagne Problems: Problems that seem trivial compared to other larger issues in the world.
Charlie Puth: American singer-songwriter.
Chateau: A French term for a grand country house or castle, often implying luxury estates like those in the Loire Valley.
Checkmate: In chess to check the opponent's king so that escape is impossible.

Chelsea Hotel: The 12-story Chelsea, originally
a housing cooperative, has been the home of numerous
writers, musicians, artists, and entertainers, some of
whom still lived there in the 21st century. As of 2022,
most of the Chelsea is a luxury hotel.

Chesire Cat: The Cheshire Cat is a fictional
cat popularized by Lewis Carroll in Alice's Adventures in
Wonderland and known for its distinctive mischievous
grin.

Circumstances: The sum of essential and environmental
factors.

Cinephile: A person who is fond of motion pictures.

Clara Bow: American actress who rose to stardom during
the silent film era of the 1920s and successfully made the
transition to "talkies" in 1929. Her appearance as a plucky
shopgirl in the film It brought her global fame and the
nickname "The It Girl".

Clandestine: Kept secret or done secretively.

Cleopatra: Queen of Egypt.

Cloaked: The past tense of "cloak," meaning concealed
or disguised, like wearing a hidden identity.

Coax: Influence or persuade someone to do something by
gentle urging, sooth talk or flattery.

Cobblestone: A small, round stone, formerly used to
cover road surfaces.

Cocky: Conceited or arrogant.

Combat: A fight or contest between individuals or
groups.

Complex: Complicated.

Conduct: To direct or take part in the operation or
management of.

Coney Island: Neighborhood and entertainment area in
the southwestern area of the New York City borough
Brooklyn.

Congressman: A member of the U.S. House of Representatives.
Consolation: The comfort received by a person after a loss or disappointment.
Contempt: Disregard for something that should be considered.
Contrarian: A person who opposes or rejects popular opinion.
Conquest: A person whose favor or hand has been won.
Convene: Come or bring together for a meeting or activity; assemble.
Cornelia Street: Song from the Lover album, refers to a street in New York City where Taylor once rented an apartment.
Counterfeit: A fraudulent imitation of something else; a forgery.
Coven: An assembly of witches.
Covert: Not openly acknowledged or displayed.
Crease: A line or ridge produced on paper or cloth by folding, pressing, or crushing.
Crestfallen: Feeling shame or humiliation, dejected.
Crimson Clover: An annual European clover that has cylindrical heads of crimson flowers and is cultivated in the U.S. especially as a cover crop.
Crusaders: Historically, medieval Christian warriors on holy quests; here, metaphorically, aggressive online mobs or critics waging moral campaigns.
Cryptic: Having a meaning that is mysterious or obscure.
Currency: Paper money in circulation; a common article for bartering.
Curtail: Reduce in extent or quantity; impose a restriction on.
Cutthroat: A competitive environment where individuals are ruthless in pursuit of success, often at the expense of others.

Cut to the bone: Reduced to the lowest possible amount.
Cynical: Believing that people are motivated purely by self-interest; distrustful of human sincerity or integrity.

Dd

Damsel in distress: The damsel in distress is a narrative device in which one or more men must rescue a woman who has been kidnapped or placed in other peril.

Dappled: Marked with spots or rounded patches.

Death by a Thousand Cuts: A form of torture and execution involving a drawn-out process of administering a series of cuts to the skin, resulting in a slow and painful death.

Death rattle: A gurgling sound heard in a dying person's throat.

Dear reader: A broad way to address formal correspondence or a group of people. Often used to reply to those who write in with their problems asking for advice.

Debut: A person's first appearance or performance in a particular capacity or role. Taylor's first album is often referred to as Debut.

Debutante: An upper-class young woman making her first appearance in fashionable society.

Delusion: A false belief or judgment about external reality, held despite incontrovertible evidence to the contrary.

Deranged: Disturbed or upset, especially mentally.

Descends: Move or fall downward.

Desertion: The abandonment without consent or legal justification of a person, post, or relationship and the associated duties and obligations.

Destin: A city in Northwestern Florida.

Devil is in the details: Idiom that means something may seem simple but in fact the details are complicated and likely to cause problems.

Discretion: The quality of being careful and restrained, especially in speech or actions to avoid scandal.

Disposition: A person's inherent qualities of mind and character.

Distraught: An adjective meaning deeply upset, agitated, or emotionally overwhelmed.

Dive Bar: A dive bar is typically a small, unglamorous, eclectic, old-style drinking establishment with inexpensive drinks.

Dog days: The hot, sultry days of summer.

Dom Perignon: A brand of vintage champagne.

Dopamine: A compound that occurs in the body, known as a feel-good hormone.

Downtown Lights: A song by the band The Blue Nile.

Dressed to the nines: To be dressed very elegantly or flamboyantly, often for a special occasion.

Drought: A prolonged period of abnormally low rainfall, leading to a shortage of water.

Dutiful: Conscientiously or obediently fulfilling one's duty.

Dwindling: Diminish gradually in size, amount, or strength.

Dylan Thomas: A Welsh poet and writer and famous resident of the Chelsea Hotel.

Dynasty: A succession of people from the same family who play a prominent role in business, politics, or another field.

Ee

Elegies: A poem of serious reflection, typically a lament for the dead.

Elizabeth Taylor: The iconic actress (1932–2011), known for her violet eyes, eight marriages, and roles in films like *Cleopatra*.

Embroider: Embellishment or exaggeration in the description or reporting of an event.

Empathetic: Showing an ability to understand and share the feelings of another.

End Game: The final stage of a game such as chess or bridge, when few pieces or cards remain.

Epiphany: A usually sudden illuminating discovery or realization.

Era: A period of one's life or career that is of a distinctive character.

Esoteric: Intended for or likely to be understood by only a small number of people with a specialized knowledge or interest:

Eulogize: Praise highly in speech or writing.

Evergreen: Relating to or denoting a plant that retains green leaves throughout the year.

Evermore: Forever, always. Name of Taylor's 9th album.

Excruciating: Intensely painful.

Exile: To expel or bar someone from their native country, typically for political or punitive reasons.

Exoneration: Legal or moral clearance from blame or accusation.

Exorcise: Rid a person or place of an evil spirit.

Ff

Fable: A short story, typically with animals as characters, conveying a moral.

Fallout: The adverse side effects or results of a situation.

Father Figure: A mature, protective male role model.

Fearsome: Frightening, especially in appearance.

Fever dream: Vivid and often bizarre dreams that occur when a person has a high fever.

Feverishly: In a frenetically excited or energetic manner.

First String: First choice players.

Fleck: Spot, flake or particle.

Flush: A reddening of the face, skin, etc., typically caused by illness or strong emotion. Having plenty of something.

Fold: To concede defeat by withdrawing from play.

Folklore: The traditional beliefs, customs, and stories of a community, passed through the generations by word of mouth.

Fortnight: A period of 14 days or two weeks.

Fraternity: A male students' society in a university or college.

Frigid: Very cold in temperature.

Frontlines: The military line or part of an army that is closest to the enemy.

Gg

Game of chance: A game in which chance, rather than skill, determines the outcome.

Gallatin Road: A real street in Hendersonville, Tennessee, where Swift grew up.

Gallows: A structure, typically of two uprights and a crosspiece, for the hanging of criminals.

Gardens of Babylon: One of the seven wonders of the ancient world.

Gatsby: The Great Gatsby is a 1925 novel by American writer F. Scott Fitzgerald. Used to describe an extravagant party scene reminiscent of those in the book.

Gauche: Lacking social polish, poise, or refinement.

Getaway Car: A car used by criminals to leave the scene of a crime.

Girlboss: A hard-working and ambitious young woman.

Glad handling: Greeting or welcoming warmly or with the appearance of warmth.

Gleaming: Bright and shiny.

Glint: A trace of emotion expressed through the eyes. A tiny bright flash of light.

Glistening: Shining with a sparkling light.

Godforsaken: Lacking any merit or attraction; dismal.

Gold Rush: A widespread move to join a market or situation that appears to offer opportunities for making a lot of money quickly. A rapid movement of people to a newly discovered goldfield.

Good Samaritan: A person who is generous in helping those in distress.

Grand Theft Auto: An action-adventure video game series.

Graveyard shift: A work shift that runs through the early morning hours, typically covering the period between midnight and 8 a.m.

Greige: Color that blends grey and beige.
Groundwork: Preparation made beforehand.
Guilty as Sin: Completely or very guilty.

Hh

Hackles: The hairs on the back of an animal's neck or back that rise when the animal is frightened or about to fight. Figuratively, the term is used to describe something that makes people angry or annoyed.

Happenstance: A circumstance that is due to chance.

Hazing: Humiliating and sometimes dangerous initiation rituals, especially as imposed on college students seeking entry into a fraternity or sorority.

Heath: British English. an area of open uncultivated land, especially in Britain.

Hearse: A vehicle for conveying the dead to the grave.

Heist: Armed robbery.

Hereby: By this means.

Heroine: A female hero.

High and dry: An idiom for being abandoned or left helpless in a difficult situation.

Highgate: A suburb of London.

High horse: Being on a high horse means having an inflated sense of self-importance or superiority.

Hipsters: Person who is aware of and interested in unconventional things.

Hits Different: An experience that affects someone in a more profound way than usual.

Hoax: An act intended to trick or dupe.

Holiday House: The name of Taylor's house in Rhode Island. Also known as High Watch or Harkness House.

Hollywood: The American movie industry; neighborhood in Los Angeles, California.

Hologram: A picture of an object showing it in three dimensions.

Honing: The act of sharpening or refining a skill through practice.

Hostile: Of or relating to an enemy; marked by malevolence.

Hothouse Flower: A person who is very fragile and vulnerable due to having been sheltered.

Hucksters: Hawker, peddler; especially one who sells or advertises something in an aggressive, dishonest or annoying way.

Ii

Illicit: Not permitted.
Implode: To break down or fall apart from within.
Implore: To ask or beg for something urgently or earnestly.
Imposition: An excessive or uncalled-for requirement or burden.
Impressionist paintings: Paintings characterized by their visible brushstrokes, open composition and emphasis on accurate depiction of light in its changing qualities.
Incandescent: White, glowing, or luminous with intense heat.
Indelible: Not able to be forgotten or removed.
Indentation: A deep recess.
Indie: Not belonging to or affiliated with a major record or film company; independent.
Indigo: A color between blue and violet in the spectrum.
Industry Disruptors: Companies, people, or forms of technology that cause significant change in an industry or market by means of innovation. They create a product, service, or way of doing things which displaces the existing market leaders.
Infamy: Notorious or scandalous fame, often undeserved.
Infidelity: Unfaithfulness in a marriage or an intimate relationship.
Ingenue: An innocent or unsophisticated young woman, especially in a play or film.
Insincerity: Not sincere, hypocritical.
Insurmountable: Incapable of being passed over, surmounted, or overcome; insuperable.

Interlopers: A person who becomes involved in a place or situation where they are not wanted or are considered not to belong.
Intertwined: Connect or link two or more things closely.
Invisible String: The invisible string theory posits that your soul mate is always present in your life path even before you have met them.

Jj

Jack: Jack Antonoff, Taylor's long-time collaborator and producer of many of her albums.
Jackals: Any of several small omnivorous canids of Africa and Asia having large ears, long legs, and bushy tails.
Jag: Slang for a Jaguar luxury car, symbolizing speed, status, and reckless thrill.
Jagged: Rough and uneven with sharp points.
James Dean: American actor, known for his good looks.
James Taylor: American singer songwriter and guitarist.
Jehovah's Witness: Member of a Christian-based new religious movement.

Kk

Kaleidoscope: A constantly changing pattern or sequence of objects or elements; An optical instrument.
Karma: A force considered as affecting the events of one's life.
Keep it 100: Slang for being completely honest and authentic.
Ken: The male version of the Barbie doll; used to refer to a non-specific man.
Kismet: A term from Persian/Urdu for destiny or fate, often romantic.

Ll

Lavender Haze: To be deeply in love with someone or in the honeymoon stages of a relationship.
Labyrinth: A maze.
Legends: Stories, not always true, that people tell about a famous event or person.
Lenox: Refers to Lenox, Massachusetts, a historic town in the Berkshires.
Leo: Leonardo DiCaprio, American actor and film producer, known for his penchant to date younger girls. Refer to The Man from The Lover album.
Levi's: A brand of denim jeans.
Levitate: To rise or float on air.
 Lighthearted: Cheerful and carefree.
Lingered: To remain or stay longer than expected, often with reluctance.
Litany: A usually lengthy recitation or enumeration; a sizable series or set.
LOML: Acronym for Love of My Life and Loss of My Life.
Long story short: An expression indicating that one is skipping unnecessary details and getting to the point.
Loose lips sink ships: Idiom that means beware of unguarded talk and serves as a warning against speaking about confidential information.
Lost in translation: To have failed to have the same meaning or effectiveness when it is translated into another language.
Lovelorn: Bereft of love. Without love.
Luck of the draw: The result of something that cannot be controlled and depends on chance.
Lucy: Lucy Dacus, American singer-songwriter and member of band Boygenius.

Lurching: Make an abrupt, unsteady, uncontrolled movement or series of movements.

Mm

Machiavellian: Marked by cunning, duplicity or bad faith. It comes from Niccolo Machiavelli's treatise.

Madison Square: Madison Square Garden, colloquially known as the Garden or by its initials MSG is a multi-purpose arena in New York City.

Magnetic: Very attractive or alluring.

Mahogany: The durable yellowish-brown to reddish-brown usually moderately hard and heavy wood of a West Indian tree that is widely used for cabinetwork and fine finish work.

Maim: Wound or injure someone so that part of the body is permanently damaged.

Maladies: Sickness, diseases or illnesses.

Manuscript: A written or typewritten composition or document.

Marjorie: Marjorie Finlay, Taylor's late maternal grandmother and opera singer.

Maroon: A dark red. Leave in isolation.

Maserati: An Italian luxury car.

Mastermind: Someone who plans and directs an ingenious and complex scheme or enterprise.

Masquerade: A social gathering of people wearing masks. To disguise oneself.

Matinee: A performance in a theater or a showing of a movie that takes place in the daytime.

Megaphone: A device for amplifying voice; metaphorically, a bold public declaration.

Melancholia: Deep sadness or gloom; melancholy.

Mercurial: A person subject to sudden or unpredictable changes of mood or mind.

Metaphor: A figure of speech that compares two different things by stating that one is the other.

Midas touch: The ability to achieve financial reward or success from one's actions easily and consistently.
Mirrorball: a revolving ball covered with small, mirrored facets, used to provide lighting effects at discos or dances.
Montage: The technique of producing a new composite whole from fragments of pictures, text, or music.
Mosaic: A surface decoration made by inlaying small pieces of variously colored material to form pictures or patterns.
Motion Capture: The process or technique of recording patterns of movement digitally, especially the recording of an actor's movements for the purpose of animating a digital character in a movie or video game.
Motown: An upbeat often pop-influenced style of rhythm and blues associated with the city of Detroit.
Muse: A source of Inspiration.
Musso and Franks: Musso & Frank Grill, a historic Hollywood restaurant (est. 1919) frequented by stars like Elizabeth Taylor and Taylor Swift.

Nn

Narcissism: Excessive love of oneself.
Narcotics: A drug that relieves pain and induces drowsiness, stupor, or insensibility.
New Heights: Travis and Jason Kelce's podcast.
Nicety: A fine detail or distinction.
Nobleman: A man of high birth or honorable character, like a knightly protector.
Nonchalant: Feeling or appearing casually calm and relaxed; not displaying anxiety, interest, or enthusiasm.
Nostalgia: A sentimental longing or wistful affection for the past, typically for a period or place with happy personal associations.
Notch in your belt: A remarkable success or achievement, especially one that adds to a successive string of accomplishments.
Novelty: A new or unfamiliar thing or experience.

Oo

Oblivion: The state of being unaware or unconscious of what is happening.

Obnoxious: Extremely unpleasant.

Odd man out: A person who differs from the other members of a group.

Old Fashioned: Refers to a drink made with whiskey.

One for the money: The start of a children's rhyme, used as a countdown before a game or a race.

One horse town: A very small town, especially one of a rural nature and/or offering very few or no attractions.

Onyx: A black gemstone symbolizing protection and strength.

Opacity: The condition of lacking transparency or translucence; opaqueness.

Opalite: A synthetic blue gem (or man-made opal variant) evoking ethereal glow.

Open-shut case: A simple and straightforward problem that can be solved easily.

Ophelia: The tragic heroine from Shakespeare's *Hamlet*, driven mad by unrequited love and drowning (suicide or accident).

Opt in: To choose to do or be involved in something.

Oracle: A person or thing regarded as an infallible authority or guide on something.

Out of the woods: Clear of danger or difficulty.

Pp

Palm d'Or: The top prize at the Cannes Film Festival, a golden palm symbolizing cinematic prestige.

Paradox: A situation, person, or thing that combines contradictory features or qualities.

Pathological: Being to a degree that is excessive, extreme or markedly abnormal.

Patriarchy: A system of society or government in which men hold the power and women are largely excluded from it.

Patron: A brand of Tequila.

Patti Smith: American singer, songwriter, poet, painter, author and photographer. She lived in the Chelsea Hotel.

Pawn: A piece in chess with the least value. On that can be used to further the purposes of another.

Pearls of wisdom: Idiom for insightful advice, often hard-earned.

Peculiar: Unusual and strange.

Pedigree: The recorded ancestry, especially upper-class ancestry, of a person or family.

Peered: To look keenly or with difficulty at someone or something.

Perilous: Full of danger or risk.

Periphery/Peripheral: The outer limits or edge of an area or object.

Persona non-grata: A person who is not welcome or favored.

Perspective: The capacity to view things in their true relations or relative importance.

Petulance: Insolent or rude in speech or behavior.

Phoenix: A legendary bird which according to one account lived 500 years, burned itself and rose alive from the ashes to live another period.

Pine/Pining: Miss and long for the return of.

Pivotal: Of crucial importance in relation to the development or success of something else.
Platonic: A relationship marked by the absence of romance.
Plaza Athénée: Hôtel Plaza Athénée, a luxurious Paris hotel.
Polaroids: A photograph taken with a Polaroid or instant camera.
Poke the bear: Deliberately provoke or antagonize someone.
Ponder: To consider something deeply and thoroughly.
Portofino: A glamorous Italian Riviera village known for celebrity yachts and cliffs.
Post-mortem: After death; an analysis or discussion of an event held soon after it has occurred.
Precipice: A very steep rock face or cliff, especially a tall one.
Precocious: Behavior or abilities indicative of early development.
Prey: An animal that is caught and killed by another for food.
Prophets: A person regarded as an inspired teacher or proclaimer of the will of God.
Prophecy: A prediction.
Propriety: Conformity to what is socially acceptable in conduct or speech.
Prose: Written or spoken language in its ordinary form.
Protégé: A person guided and mentored by an expert, often in arts.
Purgatory: In Catholic theology, a temporary state of purification after death.
Pyro: Short for pyromaniac, someone obsessed with fire; slang for a fiery personality or arsonist.

Rr

Real Madrid: The elite Spanish soccer club.

Redneck: A white person of low social status living in a rural area, especially one seen as politically reactionary and unsophisticated.

Reeling: To walk or move unsteadily.

Reign: hold royal office; rule as king or queen.

Reminiscing: Indulge in enjoyable recollection of past events.

Renegade: An individual who rejects lawful or conventional behavior.

Reputation: The beliefs or opinions that are generally held about someone or something. Name of Taylor's 6th album.

Resentment: A feeling of indignant displeasure or persistent ill will at something regarded as a wrong, insult, or injury.

Revelers/ Revelry: A person who is enjoying themselves in a lively and noisy way. Joyful or riotous merry making.

Reviled: Criticized in an abusive or angrily insulting manner.

Ricochet: To rebound off something wildly in a seemingly random direction.

Rift: A crack, split, or break in something; a serious break in friendly relations.

Riviera: A coastal region.

Rivulets: Small stream of water or other liquid.

Robert Bly: American poet.

Ronan: Single by Taylor Swift based on a blog written by Maya Thompson about her son Ronan who died of neuroblastoma.

Rosé: A type of wine with a light pink color.

Rusting: Rusting is a process that causes iron to become flaky and weak, degrading its strength, appearance and permeability.
Ruthless: Having or showing no pity or compassion for others.

Ss

Saboteurs: A person who engages in sabotage. Sabotage is to deliberately destroy, damage, or obstruct.

Saint Tropez: City in France. Location of Leonardo DiCaprio's annual Foundation Gala.

Saltbox: A frame house having up to three stories at the front and one fewer at the back with a steeply pitched roof.

Sanctimonious: Hypocritically pious or devout.

Sapphire: A precious gemstone.

Scarlet: Any of various bright reds.

Scarlet Letter: A symbol of shame. Title of a book by American writer Nathaniel Hawthorne.

Scathing: Criticize someone or something in a severely critical and unkind way.

Scheming: Make plans, especially in a devious way or with intent to do something illegal or wrong.

Screw-top: Having a top or lid that can be attached and removed by being turned.

Scrutiny: Critical observation or examination.

Scout's honor: The oath taken by a boy scout or girl scout, used to indicate that someone will stand by their promise or tell the truth.

Shooting the messenger: Metaphoric phrase used to describe the act of blaming the bearer of bad news, despite the bearer or messenger having no direct responsibility for the bad news or its consequences.

Shot in the dark: An attempt that has little chance of success.

Showgirl: A glamorous performer in lavish revues (e.g., Las Vegas dancers in feathers and sequins).

Shrouded: Covered or enveloped to conceal from view.
Slammer: Jail, prison.
Sleeper Cell: A secretive group of spies or terrorist agents that remain inactive within a target population until ordered to act.
Sleeping with the Fishes: Mafia slang for being murdered and dumped in water.
Smooth talking: Talking in a friendly and pleasant way that may not be completely honest or sincere, often used to persuade.
SoCal: Southern California.
Soliloquies: The act of a character speaking to themselves to reveal their thoughts to the audience.
Solitaire: Any of various card games played by one person.
Sorceress: A female wizard or enchantress.
Springsteen: Bruce Springsteen, American singer songwriter and guitarist.
Starlet: A young actress with a promising career ahead of her.
Starry-eyed: Naively enthusiastic or idealistic; failing to recognize the practical realities of a situation.
State of Grace: A condition of being free from sin.
Stella McCartney: English fashion designer, daughter of singer-songwriter Paul McCartney.
Stephen: From the song "Hey Stephen" is Stephen Barker Liles from the duo Love and Theft.
Stevie Nicks: American singer-songwriter known for her work with the band Fleetwood Mac.
Strategy: The art of devising or employing plans towards a goal.
Suburban: Residential community located outside the main city or town.
Sunset and Vine: The intersection of Sunset Blvd and Vine Street in Hollywood California.

Superstitious: Having a belief in supernatural influences especially as leading to good or bad luck.

Surmise: To form a thought or idea based on a small amount of evidence.

Surreal: Bizarre; Having the qualities of surrealism.

Swindle: To obtain money or property by fraud or deceit.

Sweet Nothings: Pleasant but unimportant words said by lovers. It refers to the lovey-dovey things that people in a relationship say to each other.

Synchronicity: Synchronous; happening at precisely the same time.

Tt

Tapestry: A heavy handwoven reversible textile used for hangings, curtains, and upholstery and characterized by complicated pictorial designs.

Tarnished: To dull or destroy the luster of. To bring disgrace.

Temptress: An alluring woman who seduces or exploits males.

Terminal: A condition that is incurable and irreversible and is expected to result in death.

Tendrils: A leaf, stipule, or stem modified into a slender spirally coiling sensitive organ serving to attach a climbing plant to its support.

Tethered: Fastened to something; closely connected.

The Black Dog: A pub in London referenced in TTPD song by the same name.

The Blue Nile: The Scottish electronic rock band known for suave and evocative synth arrangements, whose 1989 album "Hats" was famously a formative album for the 1975's Matty Healy, who was especially fond of the song "Downtown Lights."

The Devil you know: Shortened version of the proverb "better the devil you know than the devil you don't". It means that when faced with a difficult or undesirable choice, it is often better to stick with something familiar, even if it is bad, rather than risk the unknown.

The Lakes: Song from the Folklore album. Refers to the Lakes District in England. Many English poets lived there including William Wordsworth.

The road not taken: A poem written by Robert Frost, about choosing between two paths.

The Starting Line: American punk-pop band formed in 1999.

Thick as thieves: Having a close, intimate friendship or alliance.

Throttle: A valve for regulating the supply of fluid to an engine.

Tim McGraw: American country singer and songwriter.

Tolerate: To endure or to put up with.

Torrid: Ardent, passionate.

To the quick: To the exposed flesh, especially that which is tender.

Town Car: A full-size luxury sedan that was produced by Lincoln until 2011. The term is used to describe a large, comfortable car, with an enclosed rear seat, often driven by a chauffeur.

Transfixed: Held motionless by amazement or awe.

Treacherous: Marked by hidden dangers, hazards, or perils.

Treaties: Plural of Treaty. An agreement or arrangement made by negotiation.

TTPD: Acronym for The Tortured Poets Department.

Uu

Understudy: a person who learns another's role to be able to act as a replacement at short notice.
Underworld: The mythological realm of the dead (Greek Hades) or slang for criminal underbelly.
Unforeseen: Not anticipated or expected.
Unmoored: Insecure, confused, or lacking contact with reality.
Upstanding: Honest and respectable.
Utter: Complete, absolute.

Vv

Valiant: Possessing or showing courage or determination.

Vendetta: A series of retaliatory, vengeful, vindictive or hostile acts.

Venom: Poisonous toxin from animals like snakes; metaphorically, bitter malice or spite.

Vigilante: A person who acts outside of legal authority, often violently, to punish or avenge a crime, right a perceived wrong, etc.

Vulture: A large bird related to hawks, eagles and falcons. Can refer to a person who tries to take advantage of someone in a bad situation.

Ww

Wayward: Errant or unruly, like a wandering path.

Wasteland: An ugly, often devastated or barely inhabitable place or area.

Weary: Feeling or showing tiredness, especially because of excessive exertion or lack of sleep.

Where the spirit meets the bone: Reference to Miller William's poem "Compassion", refers to the intersection of body and soul, where death and life meet.

White collar crime: A non-violent crime of deceit or concealment, usually committed for financial gain.

Wicklow: A town in Ireland.

Wield: To have and use, such as a weapon, tool, power or influence.

William Bowery: A pseudonym or pen name used by ex-boyfriend Joe Alwyn, when he co-wrote songs with Taylor Swift.

Willow: A tree that grows near water and has long, thin, flexible branches that hang down.

Wilt: To become weaker, tired or less confident.

Wilted: Drooping or fading, like a flower losing vitality.

Windermere: The largest lake in the Lake District.

Wish list: A list of desires or aspirations.

Wisteria: A climbing plant with hanging clusters of bluish-lilac or white flowers. Widely grown on walls and pergolas.

Wonderstruck: Experiencing a sudden feeling of awed delight or wonder.

Wrath: Intense anger or divine retribution.

About the Author

Naomi Curl lives in Jacksonville, Florida and attends Duval County Public Schools. She enjoys writing, singing, acting, reading and above all else, she loves Taylor Swift.

Thank you so much for reading and supporting a young author. Please leave a book review.

For any comments, errors or suggested word additions you can reach Naomi at: swiftiedictionary@gmail.com

www.ingramcontent.com/pod-product-compliance
Lightning Source LLC
Chambersburg PA
CBHW031434250726
48656CB00002B/987